How To Sell. A Book For People That Don't Work In sales.

I0491700

This book is for people that feel "I don't need to sell"

It's the book that will help you take your business from start up to thriving very quickly.

Written by Mario. C. Lucas of BeFreeSelling.com

www.befreeselling.com

Acknowledgments

I would like to thank Ross Hunt for his honest feedback on the various drafts of my book. Thanks to Matthew Yerosimou for correcting my grammar and spelling on the first draft. Last but not least I would like to thank Serena Gasparini for her continuous encouragement to get this book finished.

Questions, comments? E-mail the author at hello@befreeselling.com

Contents

What is sales?

Selling your services or product to other people.

Why is it important?

Generate income for you and your business. Sales plays a pivotal role in the success of your business. The critical role of sale is to bridge the gap between the potential needs of your customer and the product or service that you offer.

So why can't we just get on with it?

You're an expert in your field. Whatever you do, you know it better than pretty much everybody else. Sales is something that doesn't come naturally to most people and that's okay. It can be challenging at the best of times and especially in this new world we're all facing where the working world as we know it has changed.

Why do you need this book?

This book can help you understand some of the challenges you may face in a sales environment, identify what does not work in your business, why it does not work and what steps you can take to improve it.

This book will help to fast track your success as you take your company from start-up to successful by skipping many of the basic mistakes that would be made along the way.

Who the hell are you and why should I listen to you anyway?

Good question, I'm glad you asked. I've been working in a corporate sales environment for 18 years. I've had successful years and not so successful years.

I've had different challenges to overcome in my personal and professional life and made plenty of mistakes along the way. They say the best way to learn is from your own mistakes. I've made plenty of my own and I'll be sharing them with you.

I'm not one of these people that was born a natural sales person. Everything I've achieved has come from hard work, trial and error and thousands of rejections.

I've been writing my thoughts for the last few years through journaling. Part of the challenge was making sense of all my personal ramblings and thoughts that

I had jotted down over the years without the intention of sharing with anybody else, let alone writing a book about it. In this book and on my course, I've shared some of my deepest thoughts about sales and put together this playbook.

This playbook is yours to use so you can identify what works for you and your business and repeat it for the continued success of your business and your profile.

Step 1 - Identify your why

Let's start with the basics. Let's set the foundations for your mindset. Why do you do what you do?

Before you do anything else, I want you to think about why you do what you do. Why did you start your business? Why is it important that you succeed? Who are you helping? Who are you accountable to?

I'll start you off with my why's.

1   – So I can build a successful future with my wife-to-be.

2   – So my future children are able to have the privileges and life experiences I was not able to have.

Those are my why's. Think about yours and write them down on sticky notes. Place them somewhere you can see them often. Look at them to remind yourself why you do what you do. You've started your own business.

If it was easy, everyone would do it. You'll have hard days. You'll have dark days when you think about chucking it in and not going back to work. When you feel like this, look at your why's.

Step 2 - Think about your offer

Imagine you meet an old relative. An old uncle that's getting a little forgetful in his old age. He asks you what you do for work. You've got 10 seconds to tell him before he loses concentration. What would you say?

Can you accurately convey what it is that you do in 10 seconds in a way that a 5-year-old or an 85-year-old can understand? If not, you're making it too complicated. Think about this. Trim the fat and write down what you do and test it on other people. Do they understand?

Once you've worked it out, write it down on a sticky note and put it somewhere you can see it every day. Use it to remind yourself when you get lost.

Step 3 - Who do you help?

It's important to think about who you help when running a business. Who would buy your product or service?

Who would give up their hard-earned money to buy what you have to offer? Who does your product help?

Let's use me as an example.

I help start-ups and entrepreneurs identify gaps in their sales strategy to maximize opportunities and increase their turnover.

Pretty simple right?

Think about who your business helps and write this down. Put it on a sticky note and look at it every day.

Step 4 - Who buys from you?

When targeting customers there are different things we can do –

- Build a website and hope people find it.

- Get on the phone and ring people you think might be interested.

- Go to events or roadshows and talk about y our business.

- Open a shop front and hope passers-by come in.

- Talk about your business on social media and hope the right people see it.

What's really important here is segmentation. You have to work out your ideal customer persona.

You can segment by;

Sex, age group, lifestyle, family situation, job, position, interest, political view, sexual orientation, musical taste, fashion style, disposable income and lots more.

Write it down. Who should you be targeting? When you're targeting people, you want as many people as possible to find out about your business that will actually buy and keep buying from you.

Step 5 - Who buys from you?

There are two reasons why people buy things:

- To solve a problem or a need

- For pleasure

What was the last thing you bought on Amazon?

I recently purchased a turbo trainer. Why? you might ask. Let's look into it;

Problem –

I was a bit concerned that due to the recent lockdown, I wasn't able to get out and exercise as much as I normally would. I also found that my eating habits were becoming pretty bad and I was starting to put on some weight.

Solution –

I enjoy cycling so I purchased a turbo trainer so I could get some exercise done at home.

I bought it because I had a problem I was looking to solve. I was concerned I was putting on weight and I couldn't go outside to exercise as much as I normally would.

I've got a wedding coming up in a few months' time and I was becoming concerned I wasn't looking my best.

I did what I normally do and what loads of other people do when they have a problem; I threw money at the situation.

A sales persons job is to help a customer identify their problem and show them how their product or service can solve it. It's about asking the right questions and identifying the pains and trigger points. Remember, you're not selling anything. Your job is to help them to buy.

As we said above, there are only two reasons why people buy things. Why will people buy from you?

What problems do you solve? Think about that and write it down. Knowing what problems, you solve and why people buy is the single biggest piece of advice I can give you.

If you don't know the problem your customers are trying to solve and aren't able to clearly convey that in your messaging and in every single conversation you have with a customer, you have will have a huge problem.

Step 6 – Identifying what works and what doesn't

How do you make a cup of tea? Do you put the milk in first with the teabag then pour the boiling water? Do you pour the boiling water onto the tea bag, let it brew, take the tea bag out then pour milk?

There are many ways to make a cup of tea. Some people will interpret different ways as being wrong.

There are many ways to try and sell something, you'll get some wrong and some right. Success is about identifying what works for you and what doesn't.

Having a script for different scenarios can help. Building a script is usually a case of trial and error and it depends so much on the person you're trying to appeal to and the problem you're trying to solve.

Some people wing it, but this is not a sustainable way or working and it is hard to measure what is successful in this approach. Often, these people come unstuck.

You'll need to know what to say, when to say it and the right tone to say it in. You'll need to get your passion for your brand or business across.

Make them believe in it as much as you do by sounding confident, engaging and easy to talk to. You'll need something to fall back on to lead the conversation to where you need it to go.

Step 7 - Tell a story

A well-told, captivating story can affect listeners on multiple levels. It's no accident that storytelling is a craft that has stood the test of time.

When we listen to a presentation or lecture, part of the brain that deals with language and logic is stimulated.

In contrast, when we are told a story with rich meaning and visual cues, things change dramatically. Both the right and left sides of the brain are activated. The right side (creative side) is engaged and stimulated.

A well told story can:

- Grip us and help us experience emotions.
- Capture the attention of your customer

- Motivate individuals and groups to take action

- Build trust and rapport

- Make data and facts sing by becoming applicable, interesting, and relevant

- Transform beliefs and change minds

Think of this as an opportunity to share customer testimonials. Good news stories about how people you've helped in the past have benefited from your service.

Think back to someone you've helped. What similarities do they have with the person you're speaking with now? Explain the problem they were having and how your product solved it.

Another really important tip when telling a story is to keep it really simple. The ability to convey something complicated and make it sound simple is really important. Long words just make people switch off. Nobody is impressed by them and they'll lose attention and focus quickly.

I use what I call the 'a bit like' principle. So, when you're trying to explain something technical or slightly complex, use a bit like to make it seem straight forward and relate it to something we all know. For example, if you were trying to explain Wikipedia to your 85-year-old uncle, you might say something like this:

It's an online encyclopaedia. It's a bit like the encyclopaedia's you have at home but it relies on people to keep it up to date.

The 'a bit like' principle is a valuable tool to help take your story telling and sales game up significantly.

Step 8 - I object, your honour

When you're considering making a purchase or committing to something, do you ever get a doubt in your mind? We all do. It's rare that you'll approach a potential customer with an opportunity and they don't say "no" at some point during the sale.

In fact, it's pretty much unheard of. But, giving up at the first objection won't get you very far. Now it's important here not to think or worry that you'll come off as a pushy sales person.

View objections as an opportunity to start a conversation about your service. Think about the following:

- Never be disappointed with an objection. This will switch people off.
- Never feel defensive, be confident in your solution.

- You can challenge an objection without it being a confrontation

- Most objections fall in to the categories of; they need more information, they need more justification, their needs have not yet been met.

- The majority of the time objections are just questions.

Try to understand the objection and keep going. It's all part of the fun.

Step 9 – Talk about it... and don't push it

Good selling is about good communication.

Sales people have historically been seen as sleazy and untrustworthy. The reality is that couldn't be further than the truth. A pushy approach will actually turn the customer away.

Focus on value and helping your customer solve a problem they have.

Think about the way you communicate and talk about your product. The passion you have for something you've created and let this shine through in your conversations and communications with your customer.

Step 10 – Get it out there

In step 4 we discussed how you get your product out there in front of potential buyers. A method we haven't touched on is social media. The explosion of social selling over the last 5 years has been nothing short of incredible.

The level of analysis people can do now when making a purchasing decision is like nothing we've ever seen before. Reputation is also important as any bad experiences people have had in the past can come back to bite you hard by way of a review.

It's important to be active on social media in 2020 and there are a number of platforms that allow you showcase your brand and products.

Twitter – A character limit of 280 means you have little to play with to get your idea's across. However, Twitter is excellent for giving quick bites of information on what you're up to and answering customer queries. You might even be lucky enough to get an influencer retweet you which will bring your brand to the attention of potentially millions of followers.

Potential reach – 386m active users.*

Instagram – A photo and video sharing applicating people usually access through their mobile phone. You can upload photo's or videos and share them with friends and followers. It also allows people to leave comments. For many businesses Instagram is a fantastic tool for targeting people in a select area or interest via hashtags.

Potential reach – 1 billion active users.*

Facebook – Initially we probably signed up to Facebook to keep in touch with friends and family. Then people started creating business pages and groups and all of a sudden it became the number one way to target customers. Almost a third of the people on planet earth have a Facebook account and use it regularly. People use it to share so much information that being able to dissect and target a specific sub set of people has never been easier.

Potential reach – 2.5 billion active users.*

There are other platforms such as Pinterest. Reddit, Snapchat, TikTok, LinkedIn and a few that target the Asian market specifically. Each one will have its advantages and its worth looking into in great detail.

My advice here would be to not try and have an active presence on all the platforms. Unless you're paying a social media agency to do this for you, it can take up a lot of your time. I'd pick 2/3 and really dedicate time to make sure you get right. The 2/3 that you do pick should be the ones where your customers spend most of their time and focus. Demographic statistics are widely available online so use this to determine which platforms to spend your time on.

Post regularly and keep your customers informed on what you're up to as well as special offers.

Towards the back of this book you'll find a bonus section on Social Selling via LinkedIn.

*Source - https://datareportal.com/social-media-users

Summary

Thanks for reading. Followed closely, the advice above will help you feel more comfortable about selling.

Please visit our website www.befreeselling.com for more information. Regular updates and information on our regular free webinars and information on our Be Free Selling Incubator system.

This will help you take your sales game into the stratosphere.

Bonuses

Articles and blogs

In this special edition of How To Sell, we've included some bonus material. A selection of specific articles written with actionable insights to help you do your job better.

You'll find more articles and blog posts on our website – www.befreeselling.com

Three ways to build trust

How many times has it happened to you? You walk through the doors of a place of business and here he comes – perfectly groomed with a smile planted across his face in greeting.

Within two minutes he has talked non-stop and promised you everything, including the stars if you purchase his project. You lift and eyebrow, and think to yourself... "Yeah, right!"

The distrust between consumer and salesman is a longstanding feeling. After all, you know they are wanting to make a buck off your purchase. Sure, you don't mind them making a few dollars... everybody has to make a living... but heck, it would be nice if they were at least a little concerned about what your needs are too!

Let's face it... customers aren't likely to buy from you unless they feel confident that you will deliver. There are a few easy steps that you can take to give them the confidence they need to take the plunge.

1. Let Previous Customers Make the Claim

The proof is in the pudding... No one can say that you deliver and make good on your promises like a satisfied customer. It pays to use customer testimonials. Now, we're not talking about blindly pasting testimonials everywhere... a little business sense and organization will be helpful in making the most of them.

Choose testimonials that are exact and talk about specific aspects of your business. "Thank you so much for your hard work!" is wonderful, but "Thank you for spending 2 hours with me yesterday. Your personal attention is greatly appreciated." says a lot more. Yeah, the reader knows that you are willing to take whatever time it takes to help them through the purchasing process.

Be sure to get your customer's permission to use their testimonial as part of your advertising campaign. While you're at it, get as much personal information about them as you can. Their occupation, city, etc., create a more realistic appeal to their testimony.

2. Be Specific In Your Claims

Specific claims are more believable than vague, generic brags. Order today! It's Fast, Easy and Cheap! Sounds much better when you say... Order Today! Take 2 Minutes to Fill Out Our 7 Step Order Form and Save 20% on Your Purchase!

Specific numbers don't always come out even. In fact, readers tend to believe numbers that have decimals are more accurate than whole numbers... even if the real number is exactly a whole number!

3. Be Realistic

Don't alienate customers with claims that sound too good to be true. Yeah, we all know the old saying that if it sounds too good to be true, it probably is. Unrealistic claims steal your credibility and leave the customers with a raised eyebrow.

Think of it this way... what if you do understate the benefits? When your customer finds out the truth, he'll just be that much more satisfied! Marketers suggest that you under promise and over deliver to create the greatest customer satisfaction.

Customers who believe in you aren't afraid to buy from you. That means higher sales numbers and greater profit.

The 80/20 rule

Would you believe that 80% of your sales most likely come from 20% of your customers? The reality is that this is undoubtedly the case for the majority of businesses, small and large. This means that more than likely, your next sale will come from someone who has already done business with you.

Back in 1906, Vilfredo Pareto learned that 80% of Italy's wealth was held by only 20% of the people. Then one day, after examining his garden, he also realized that 20% of his pea pods accounted for 80% of his pea crop yield that year. Was there a lesson here? This got him thinking, and not long after, the "Pareto Principle" was established. With the same preciseness, this same principle can be applied to business. You may know it as the 80/20 rule.

This little-known principle sheds a lot of understanding on how businesses should be run. Rather than putting all your energy into new business, you would be wise to spend a reasonable amount of your time following up and servicing people who have already given you business. After all, you've already removed the first barrier. Upselling current customers should come naturally? as long as you are proactive in following up and providing top-notch service.

What does this mean to you?

Imagine, about one-fifth of your customer base is just waiting for you to offer them something new. So if you're not following up with your existing customers, you're actually passing up 80% of your potential business. Of course, if you originally provided a poor experience, this may not be the case, but for businesses that operate on a principle of integrity, this should be a natural course.

Think of it. You've probably already invested heavily in getting that first piece of business? planning, advertising, promotional activity. Now it's time to develop their "lifetime value." There's lot of things you can do to show appreciation:

Christmas and birthdays: a great time to send over a thoughtful gift or Email.

Attend events: if your customer holds annual charity events or some sort of meeting, make sure you take the time to attend and show your support.

Renewals: a great time to touch base with a notice of renewal that expresses your heartfelt appreciation for their business.

Incentives: put your money where your mouth is and show your customers' value. A gift incentive or discount can go a long way in terms of future revenues.

Touch base: call your customers every so often to see how they are doing, how the product / service you sold them is performing and inquire or listen for any other needs. Use newsletter subscriptions to keep you top-of-mind.

Great service: the single-best way to ensure customers will remain loyal. Go above and beyond. You'll be surprised at how much of an advocate that customer can turn out to be in terms of referrals.

Make sure you offer them more products / services that will meet real needs. If they liked you and the product they bought, they'll buy from you again. The important thing is to always endeavor to meet the needs of your existing and future customers.

The Possibilities are Endless!

Why we're scared to sell and how to overcome it

So, you have set up your business, got all your stationery printed, got the premises and office sorted and now you have to get out there and sell!

Suddenly you break into a cold sweat but you persevere, pick up the phone or approach your first customer and it all goes horribly wrong! This really sets you up for the next one!

The fear of selling is something which most first-time business owners suffer from. Selling is not something we are taught in school or shown by our parents (unless you are immersed in business from an earlier age!) and so the whole process is alien to us.

In this article we are going to look at exactly why we have this fear of selling and what you can do to overcome it.

But first of all what is fear?

One great definition I have heard is that fear stands for False Evidence Appearing Real. That really sums up what fear is our mind has gathered all this evidence to back up our inner doubts. This evidence is usually false but to our conscious mind it appears real and so translates into fear!

At the end of the day, our fears are mainly thoughts and thats it! When our fears grab hold of us we find every excuse under the sun not to do something to get a sale I'll ring again because it's too early/lunch time/too late, I wont approach them now; they dont look in a good mood, I have a feeling that it's not the right time to get in touch may be next week.

Sound familiar?

With these blockers getting in the way, your business will never take off! This is why you have to conquer those fears. But what are our main fears when it comes to selling and how can they be overcome?

Fear of failure

Undoubtedly top of the list for any first time (and some experienced sales people!) is the fear of failure. We never like to fail, especially in a success-orientated environment. When we do, it makes the task even harder next time round. In school we are taught to fear failure (remember all those tests when the results were read out for all the class to hear?) and this stays with us in our adult life. Success has one fatal enemy and that's the fear of failure!

But, don't be like Homer Simpson when he tried to console his son Bart who had failed in his bid to be class president; "you tried and you failed. The lesson is to never try."

So, what can you do to conquer your fear of failure?

The bottom line is that you need a rock-solid positive attitude. You must have an inner voice which is continually pushing you onto the next prospect and saying; **"come on, let's find the one who's going to say yes!"**

Failure has to be seen as a learning opportunity. In every failure, there is a nugget of information, which next time, can point you in the direction of better success. James Dyson, the inventor of the revolutionary vacuum cleaner, summed up the need for a positive attitude, when he said, "Success is made up of 99% failure."

You galvanise yourself and you keep going as a full optimist.

Image Fears

We all have the image of a successful salesperson;
self-confident, well dressed, good communicator,
knowledgeable. We are our own worst critic and
we quickly see the supposed flaws in our
characters, which are either not there, or are so
small that most people cannot detect them. Yet
we allow our poor self-image to drag us down. We
convince ourselves that we cannot sell. Unless you
are confident about your own ability to sell then
the task is twice as hard.

Remember that you are not born with confidence
it's something we learn!

Not everyone has boundless self-confidence.
When you start out in business, there is
sometimes a nagging doubt that you may have
bitten off more than you can chew. This inner
doubt chips away at your self-confidence and soon
you have a poor self-image, which reflects in your
sales pitch. To be a successful salesperson you

have to have a strong self-image. To improve your self-image, follow these steps:

- Write down the qualities which you believe a successful salesperson should possess. Try and limit the list to 4 or 5 key qualities.

- Find a quiet spot and relax your body and mind with deep and steady breathing. Once you are totally relaxed recite the strong, self-image qualities you identified earlier.

- Imagine or visualise yourself possessing each of these qualities. See in your mind's eye how you look, now that you have these qualities. See how successful you are, how you look, and the car you are driving, where you are living.

- Repeat to yourself that you are assuming each of these qualities and becoming a better person with each day that passes

- Repeat this exercise first thing in the morning and last thing at night and you'll soon find your self-image and confidence levels increasing!

Fear of Rejection

No one likes to hear the word No!

The fear of rejection is another major stumbling block some people have to overcome when selling. Sometimes the fear of rejection is so big that their whole sales presentation is overshadowed. Their subconscious is saying "Why are you bothering?"

You know they are going to say no!

The presentation gets even worse; words are mumbled and product features are forgotten.

The result?

You get a No!

Hearing the response, "No" is not a great motivator! The main way to deal with rejection is just to accept that it happens. Try and re-frame any rejection you get by saying to yourself that it's the customer who loses out, not you. Walk away with a smug smile on your face and remind yourself that you are one step closer to someone who will say Yes.

Product Knowledge Fears

Successful selling can only be achieved if you know your product or service inside out. If you don't know all the features and benefits how can you ever hope to persuade someone that your product can solve all their problems? You may have had one bad experience where a customer highlighted your lack of knowledge but for some reason you have not put it right. Your subconscious continues to recognise this weakness and does what it can to sabotage your future presentations!

A lack of in-depth knowledge about your product or service quickly finds its way to making for a poor presentation. There is only one solution and that's to get learning!

Absorb yourself in the product. Understand all the features and benefits, so that you can confidently talk about all aspects of your offering. Banishing this fear is one of the easy ones to put right.

Fear of Criticism

No one likes being criticised for what they do!

We may do something to the best of our ability but our self-confidence soon disappears when someone criticises our selling style or product. This links in with the fear of a poor self image. If you have a low self-image then criticism can hurt even more. On the other hand, people with a high self-image can usually bounce back from a critical comment.

If you carry out the exercises on improving your self-image, your ability to take criticism will also improve. Decide to view criticism more as feedback than a direct attack on you. There is usually some element of truth in the majority of critical comments and it's important that you take the opportunity to learn and change.

Presentation Fears

You may be aware that your presentation skills leave a lot to be desired! Your sales pitch may be all over the place and lack any real structure, resulting in an inability to get the customer to commit. Your lack of confidence quickly shows up and the customer walks off with his wallet firmly in his pocket. This fear all boils down to lack of training. If you can spot this weakness or fear, then you are half way there. Most sales people don't even know they have a training problem!

Your presentation fear can be down to a lack of structure around your sales process. Write a basic outline on how you wish a perfect sales pitch to go. Prepare a script for the key parts of the presentation and rehearse, rehearse, rehearse!

Why not ask someone to help you role play a sales presentation?

This will give you the opportunity to make all the mistakes you want but in a risk-free environment! You should also visit befreeselling.com and see what courses they are running on sales skills.

Effective sales training and the actions above will assist in improving your confidence and result in a more professional sales presentation.

Selling does not have to be a fearful experience! If you have the right attitude, a strong self-belief, a full understanding of your product and plenty of practice, then you will have nothing to fear. So, take a look at each of these fears and put a plan in place to tackle them today!

The Power of Asking

People say to me, Mario, I am creating brochures and I am meeting people. I am telling people about my business and I just don't seem to be getting anywhere.

Do you have any suggestions?

When I say to them, "have you asked them to buy your product or service?" I quite often get a blank stare back at me. "Ask??" You mean I should ask?

Yes, this is a very important part of doing business, and many people have lost sales that they would have received if they had only asked for the sale.

This is called, **the close.**

Some people have said, "But what if they say no?"

So what?

The odds are in business that you will have more no's than yes's. You see, the more that I have studied marketing, the more I see how true that is. Just consider the no's practice on your way to a yes.

Some of the most successful marketers and sales people out there state that a 10% conversion is good. That means 90% were either not interested or were unable to purchase at this time due to a large variety of reasons.

No doesn't mean the end of the world or the end of your business, it just means at this moment they are not interested, and that's okay.

Ask yourself, how many sales do you believe that you will get if you don't ask. Not asking is considered the same as leaving money on the table.

Sometimes it means, you just haven't shown them a benefit that they can relate to or built enough value.

I have seen examples of people who have changed just a word or two on their web copy or their script and then the sales started pouring in.

If you need to learn how to ask for the sale there are many resources online or you can go to www.befreeselling.com where we will be running various programs on how to close.

There are countless articles, books and courses on closing a sale and if you haven't read any of them, I would highly recommend that you do. They go into detail on the early close, the trial close and the final close. As well, I have seen different names given to different styles.

Sadly, the reality is, many people have a sales phobia and would rather socialize at networking event and hope someone will come up and buy their product or service. And believe it or not, other people may think yes, it is a good product but you are apparently just showing me today.

So, if the word sales drives you into a frenzy then start by reading, "The Aladdin Factor" by Jack Canfield and Mark Victor Hansen. It is a book on how to ask for and get what you want in every area of your life. And, has in it a formula for overcoming the seven most common "asking fears"

It is important to remember that *no matter what business you are in, you are always selling yourself*, product and or service and knowing how to do it well will assist and help your clients. When you have a valuable product or service that improves people's lives, consider it your obligation to let them know that it exists.

You will feel more confident than approaching them as though you are a pest. Just remember, it's your job to ask and it's ok if they say no.

Smile and go on to the person just waiting for your arrival.

Goal Setting

There was a time when five-year plans were all the rage. But that was when workers can still count on signing up with a company for life. In the warp-speed world of technology, five years is an eternity. So how is one supposed to map out one`s career when the business landscape is always changing?

Firstly, *a plan is useless but planning is still essential.* Instead of a five-year plan, try formulating a five-year vision. In that way, you can chart a course you would like to follow.

For example, today I am on the team; in two years, I would like to be managing it; in three years, I would like to be relocated to build a new team in a new market; and in five years, I would like to be coordinating a group of international teams. Just keep in mind that the course will almost certainly change.

Secondly, workers should not confine their career projections within the framework of their current companies as they did previously. Instead, they should understand that while it is beneficial to set a goal of being a supervisor in five years, you might need to move to another company in another country to achieve it. Construct a portfolio of your achievements and market yourself by including your personal goals along with your career goals. It is important to include financial planning, as one cannot rely on employers` plans to manage one`s money.

Thirdly, workers should identify employment-related characteristics regardless of other factors. The key to planning is for workers to upgrade their own skills and stay relevant in the job market. This applies strongly to the engineering profession. For the first four to five years, the engineer`s plan will be broken into two major periods. The first two years will be learning key technical training and after that the engineer will be placed in the field for a couple of years. The engineer should take advantage of all opportunities to try out different aspects of engineering during these five years. After this incubation period, the engineer would need to be flexible and able to chart his own course, even into overseas countries with strong career growth opportunity.

Fourthly, workers should make their plans incremental and somewhat aggressive. This is very much the case in creative fields such as design and architecture. Creative people are expected to do rather than wait to be told what to do. But even the most creative businesses are businesses at heart. So, a career plan for a designer or decorator should include delving into the business side of projects.

In general, you must first decide what specific path you wish to take, and then proceed down that road ambitiously, scooping up opportunities when they appear. Long-term plans can be used as guides, but they become folly if they are followed rigidly.

Set your goals. Map out a plan. Create a vision. Then six months later, be ready to rethink those goals.

Goal Setting II

Every person should write down his or her goals. Business goals, personal goals, income goals, and whatever you want to achieve in your life. If you want to achieve something in your life, don't just think about it. Get a nice piece of paper and write down the goal. Put it somewhere you see it every day.

Having a goal sitting in your head may not help that much. Every book says that you need to write down your goals. First thinking about the goal is a good way to start but again, you need to write it down as soon as you think about it.

What is it that you want to accomplish?

Think about this in your mind and come up with the exact goal that you want to get. For example, let's look at a person who wants to earn $1000 in the next 30 days online. Here is what he or she needs to do.

The first step is to write down the goal of earning $1000 in the next 30 days. So that's done. Good.

Next what you will want to do is to write how you are going to achieve this goal. You should figure out by now that you will want to find someone who has already done this before. Having a burning desire will also help you get to your goal.

Write down why you want to achieve this goal. For some, it is just having that extra income to help them pay for a car payment. For others, it may be that they want to save money. Whatever your goals are, write down **why** you want to achieve them.

Another point to consider is to have complete faith in yourself and your desired goals. You need to have faith because if you don't, you may not achieve your goals at all. You may have written them down, but it means nothing if you kick out your belief of achieving this goal from your "belief" system that is sitting there somewhere in your head. You need to have faith that you can reach any goal that you set.

After you achieve a particular goal, don't forget to give yourself a pat on the back. Give yourself some sort of a reward. Once you achieve your first goal, you can accomplish any of your future goals in life. It should give you some sort of motivation to write more and more goals down.

Now, what would happen if you don't reach your goal? This can happen to anyone who sets goals. The best thing that you will need to do is to learn from this situation and think what you can do next time to achieve that goal.

If you fail once, try again. If you fail the second time, then try again until you reach your desired goal. But don't take the same action. Learn what you did wrong in the first trial and try something different.

Public Speaking & Presenting

If you're trying to sell a product, its inevitable that at some point you're going to have to speak to an audience. This is something that didn't come naturally to me and my first few attempts were, let's just say, a complete shambles.

Talking about your business is one thing. You can prepare a script and let's face it, nobody knows your business better than you, right?

But what about when you get questions from the audience? For some people this is a huge fear as its completely unscripted and you have no control over what people are going to ask you.

How you handle questions from an audience can often be the deciding factor as to how your presentation is received. If you're pitching for business, then it's absolutely vital to handle questions well.

These top tips will help:

1. Be prepared for questions – When you write your presentation, think about what you're likely to be asked and what your answer is going to be. Maybe you won't want to answer a particular question there and then, so think about what you'll say to satisfy the questioner.

2. Make it clear at the start – You may decide to take questions as you go or at the end of your presentation. Whatever you decide, make it clear at the start and don't change your mind. I would suggest questions at the end in a short presentation; if you take questions as you go, then your timing will get knocked out. And always remember, an audience won't forgive you for taking half an hour when you were only scheduled to speak for fifteen minutes.

3. Never finish with questions – Far better to ask for questions five or ten minutes before the end, deal with the questions and then summarise for a strong finish. Too many presentations finish on questions and the whole thing goes a bit flat – particularly if you don't get any.

4. Listen – When asked a question, listen and look like your listening. It may be something you've heard a million times before. Treat the questioner with respect and don't trivialise their point.

5. Thank the questioner – It's only polite, it shows respect and it gives you a bit more time to consider your answer. There's a famous video of Steve Jobs getting a question from an audience member when introducing one of the new Apple products. To give himself time to think and formulate a response, he took a long sip of water. This

method made also made him super cool and composed.

6. Repeat the essence of the question – Some people may not have heard the question so your answer may not make any sense to them. It can also be irritating for them not to hear the question. Again, it gives you more time to think of the answer and it makes you look so clever and in control.

7. Answer to everyone – Don't fall into the trap of only answering the questioner. If they happen to be near the front then you could end up having a conversation with them and exclude everyone else.

8. Keep it simple – Many speakers, when it comes to questions, have become more relaxed and the fact that someone is interested enough to ask them a question, leads them to go on too long with the answer – DON'T.

9. Don't bluff or bluster – If you don't know the answer to a question, say so and find out. Suggest to the questioner that you'll 'phone them or come and see them with the answer. It can even be a good way to make further contact after the presentation. Don't feel like you have to answer a question just because you were asked.

As we all know, it's possible that you may not be asked any questions and you then have that awkward silence. People may be thinking about what you've just said and may need more time to ask. They may also be a bit shy and may take a few minutes to speak out. Why not have a question of your own prepared and say something like. "You may be asking yourself.........?" If you still fail to get any questions then go straight into your summary and closing statement.

Handling a question and answer session well, demonstrates your professionalism and reflects on your message.

Million Dollar Emails

The world has definitely changed since I started in the world of sales.

There was no Facebook, no LinkedIn or Instagram. Twitter was merely a spark in Jack Dorsey's eye. People were moving away from fax machines (remember those??) and email was becoming the primary form of communication between businesses.

Things have changed a lot.
The way we communicate with our friends and family has changed significantly during this time. I remember growing up and all we had was a house phone and teletext.

The evolution of the smartphone has changed everything. We now have computers glued to us that are more powerful than most PC's could only dream about 10 years ago. And with that, the way we communicate and do business has changed. Gary Vee always says, go where the attention is. And people's attention is on their mobile phone. The way people buy has changed.

When you last booked a vacation, how did you do it? Chances are, you didn't walk into a travel agency. A recent study by compareholidaymoney.com found that 80% of holidays are now booked online.

So, what does this mean for you and your business?

The way you approach customers and find new business has to change for you to truly meet your sales targets and grow your business, fast. Building up a presence on social media is now imperative.

Customers are now doing their own research. They like to buy and not be sold to. Having a strong social media profile gives you social proof. Back in school, the good-looking athletic types were always the most popular. You'd want to be seen with them as that would enhance your own social profile. It's exactly the same in business now. Just sending messages on LinkedIn and cold emails is not enough.

You have to put the work in on building a brand that people want to associate themselves with.

Be an authority on the topic at hand. Be the go-to business to solve a particular need the customer has.

Provide value to the customer and that will create endless opportunities for your business in the future. I like to use the term – give, give, give, give and ask.

Your profile on social media is so important. Use Instagram to provide examples of your work. Use Twitter to provide your thoughts and opinions. Use LinkedIn to Network and use Facebook for all three. These are the platforms your customers will use to do their own research. Make sure you're active and available.

Think about your buyers and where their attention is.

In my first book – How to Sell – I told you about customer segmentation. Think carefully about who might give you business and your ideal customer and where their attention is. That platform is where you want to put most of your focus.

In this book, I will give you some examples of outreach on LinkedIn. I have used LinkedIn effectively for the last 5 years to build a personal social profile which has resulted in people approaching me regularly to provide them with whatever service the business I am working for at the time offered.

What LinkedIn is not.

The use of LinkedIn as a business 2 business sales platform has exploded over the last 5 years and in my opinion is set to grow even more over the next 5. There really is no other platform like it for professional networking.

The power of a connection request and message on LinkedIn at the moment is incredibly high. How else can you, an entrepreneur, get a direct line to the CEO of a multinational corporation, politician or key contact at pretty much any business in the world? 10 years ago this would have been unheard of. But, getting their attention is not easy. They'll get hundreds of messages and connection requests every week. These people have the buying power to change the destiny of any business in the world. They're not going to give their attention away very easily.

Using LinkedIn to spam people is not a good idea. A cut and paste message can be easily be seen through and ignored however good your product is. It's also not an opportunity to spam your connections walls with sales messages and information about your product. You'll get removed, blocked or hidden quicker than anything and you'll be wondering why you're getting no engagement.

The truth is – *nobody really cares.*

Now, that might sound harsh, but its true. Nobody truly cares about the success of your business apart from you. Your messages and content will be ignored and you'll be scratching your head asking why.

LinkedIn is also not an opportunity to connect with someone and just hit them straight away with a sales message. There's no bigger turn off and you'll lose that prospect for good. Use it as an opportunity go engage in conversation and build credibility and rapport.

So, what can you do about it?

Good question!

A strong personal and business profile is the first thing. But how do you get one of those?
Well, sharing content is a start. But, what's really powerful is getting your own content and opinions out there. This is how you become an authority in your field.

But, what do you mean?

I spent the last 8 years of my career selling software. The main buyers were IT Directors of large multinational companies. With headquarters all over the world.

When an IT Director from a company I was targeting in Canada produced some content about something business critical, there's a very high chance that an IT Director for a company in the same industry that I am targeting in the UK is going to be interested in what they have to say. Sharing that content to your followers or in a direct message, I think is a good idea. You've given them something for free that they'll find useful and you haven't even had to come up with it yourself. Getting the above right is a fantastic way to get noticed and even to get potential customers approaching you to find out more about your business or product. But outreach is still key. Approaching potential customers on LinkedIn is going to be critical to getting meetings and increasing the number of people that give up their money for your service.

In this book, I'm going to give you 20 examples of outreach messages to try on LinkedIn and where they can be useful.

Try them, tweak them but importantly, send them.
Connection requests

Personalize them. Whenever you try to connect
with someone on LinkedIn, you'll get the option to
personalize the message. It's a good idea. A
personal message is MUCH more likely to get read
an accepted.

Even something like:
Hi ****, I'd love to connect.
Is better than nothing. Keep it simple and
personal.

The most important thing before you read on.

Nobody likes SPAM

Each message you're about to read needs to be
personalized and relevant to the person you're
sending it to.

Individualize it and make it clear you've put some
thought into it and you know exactly who they are
and not a copy and paste job.

The whole point of most of these messages is to start a conversation and dialogue between you and your potential customer. I would be surprised if anybody has ever received a sales pitch on LinkedIn and thought "what a great message, let me buy exactly what they're selling" it just doesn't happen so just keep this in mind.

1 –
Hi ****, thanks or liking my article. Hopefully you found it useful; I'd love to know your thoughts on the subject?
Kind regards

You can use this example when you write an article or share some content and someone clicks like. They've already engaged with you so are very likely to respond.

2 –
Hi ****,
Thanks for accepting my connection request. I run **** and we are one of the most innovative suppliers of **** in the US. I'd love to know what **** uses for that.

Thanks again.

A great example of cold outreach once someone has accepted your connection request. Once they reply, its tempting to send loads of information about your business or product. Refrain. Build the conversation and value.

3 –

*Hi ****.*

*I run a business called **** and we (insert what you do and how you help people). If I can ever be of assistance to you, please get in touch.*

Kind regards

This is a friendly introduction. You're not asking for anything. Just letting them know that you're there.

4 –

*Hi ****

*I wanted to get in touch to let you know that we're working with (enter name of competitor) and helping them with ****. I'm conscious we've never spoken. Let me know if it's something of interest.*

This is great way to get a meeting. The right prospect will be intrigued and want to know what the competition is doing.

5 –

Hi ****
Thanks for connecting.
I have a lot of contacts in (insert industry) and many of them tell me they have a problem with ****. Hopefully this problem doesn't apply to you but if it does, please let me know and hopefully we can help.

This lets them know you're a problem solver. It might be a problem they've never even thought of. The whole point of this is to get them curious and you'll, of course, let them know more.

6 –

Hi ****
I run a business called **** and we help ****. I've put together a 2.5-minute video to show how we help similar companies to you. (insert link here). Hopefully you get a chance to watch it. Please let me know what you think if you do.
Video is a fantastic tool for getting your message out there. Putting together a short video on YouTube with a simple message about what you do will help get your message out there quickly and in a medium which almost everyone uses.

There is a tool called Vidyard which allows you to record video and share your screen at the same time. You can use this to send a personalized message to your prospect. This way, they can see you and get confidence in who they're speaking to.

7 –

LinkedIn now allows you to send voice messages to your connections. This is still underused and will differentiate you from all the other crappy messages clogging up their InMail.
Use it to introduce yourself and what you do. Convey confidence and people will be intrigued and a reply is likely.

8 –

Hi ****
Recently we worked with (competitor name) and we helped them achieve ****. I've put together a case study which I think you'll find useful as we may be able to help you achieve something similar. Would you mind if I sent it to you?

This will make your prospect curious. They'll want to know what the competition is doing and if there's a trick they're missing. People are always looking for reviews on things they're considering purchasing so having a review from a competitor is a valuable tool.

9 –

Hi ****

I run **** and we help businesses like yours to ****.

We've just written an ebook about **** and I think you'll find it useful. Can I send you a copy?

You're providing free content and gaining their permission to email them. If the ebook addresses a challenge they have, they'll know where to come.

10 –

Send them a letter and follow up with a message like this –

Hi ****

It's **** from ****. Did you get my letter this week? Hopefully it reached you, I know the mail can be quite slow. I'd like to arrange a call with you to talk about it. What's the best number to reach you on?

People don't really send letters anymore. Sending a well-crafted and personalized letter outlining your offer can be very powerful. Just don't expect a letter back. Which is why following up on LinkedIn afterwards is a great idea.

Okay, that sounds great but what if they don't reply?

Well, its highly likely that will be the case. Almost all outreach messages will go unseen or ignored. But that's no excuse not to do it. You're approaching important people that have great influence and spending power to grow people's businesses. They probably don't have time to read all their messages.

So, what do you do?

Follow up. Send another message in case they missed the first one. Don't just sit there and wait. You can also pick up the phone and try and reach them that way. People's attention is spread thin these days. There are many ways to make contact and you have to find the way to approach that person and the right time. And that often means, coming at them and trying to get their attention in many different ways at the same time.
I hope you enjoyed this short book and it has given you some ideas about how to approach people on LinkedIn.

The key points I hope I got across are –

Be consistent.
Start conversations.
Don't lead with a solution or product.

Thank you very much for reading.
Please visit our website www.befreeselling.com
for more information and details about our
Incubator selling course.
M.C. Lucas

One final thank you ..... to YOU, the reader!

Thank you again for buying this book. It always makes me so happy to meet people like you that want to learn how to grow their business and ensure it becomes a success.

Your passion inspires me and many others. Thank you.

You can find out more about, my speaking and training at www.befreeselling.com

Happy selling. Remember, you're just one sale away from greatness.

www.ingramcontent.com/pod-product-compliance
Lightning Source LLC
Chambersburg PA
CBHW021457210526
45463CB00002B/807